This Book Belongs

_____

This book is dedicated to my children - Mikey, Kobe, and Jojo.

Elon Musk

By Mary Nhin

Pictures By
Yuliia Zolotova

When I was your age, I played video games.
But I also read books. A WHOLE lot of books.

I was a book junkie!

Growing up, I was bullied.

One time, some kids pushed me down a stairway. It was so bad, I even had to go to the hospital. But I didn't let that stop me from dreaming of what I could be one day.

```
1   /*              This ··;//          //—
2   *            //
3   *  //
4          window = ()r
            var x = new
    ···                           ,len =
        for(varj = 0
```

I found an interest in computers and wanted to learn how to code. Coding is the language computers speak. So guess what I did to learn more about it?

I read through a manual I found and taught myself how to code.

When I was 12, I created a space fighting game called *Blastar*. It was really cool.

I sold it to a magazine company for $500. One of my first business ventures!

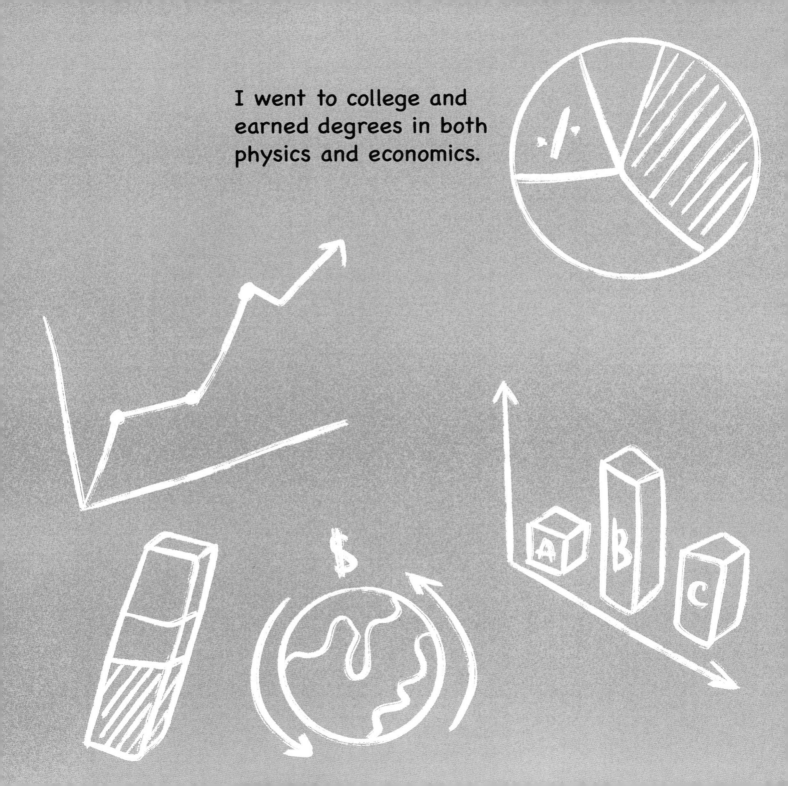

I went to college and earned degrees in both physics and economics.

After graduation, I launched a business with my brother, Kimbal. It was a company called Zip2. It provided city travel guides to newspapers like The New York Times and Chicago Tribune.

While we were building the company, I developed my hard work ethic. I worked so many hours, I basically lived at the office and showered at the local YMCA.

I kept telling myself that the hard work would be worth it one day...

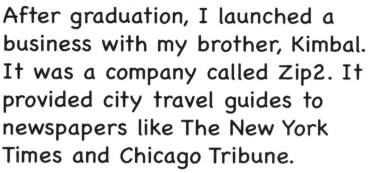

Failure is an option here. If things are not failing, you are not innovating enough.

It was worth it.

We later sold the company for a cool $426 million.

After that, I began to look for something new to invent. I found it in the finance industry. I started an online payment company which would eventually be known as Paypal. Today, more than 346 million PayPal accounts exist.

With those earnings, I reinvested some of my profits into a new invention - SpaceX, a rocket company. I wanted to send mice to Mars. My goal was to make flying to space affordable.

The first step is to establish that something is possible; then probability will occur.

Our first attempt at launching a rocket failed. So, we tried again. The rocket failed for a second time, and a third...

Actually, I failed a lot. But I did not give up. My team and I learned from our mistakes...

and we were
finally successful.

My inventions didn't stop there.
I invented things like...

fast cars that needed charging like your phone...

devices that can be implanted inside the human brain...

and a hyper-loop train that traveled super fast...

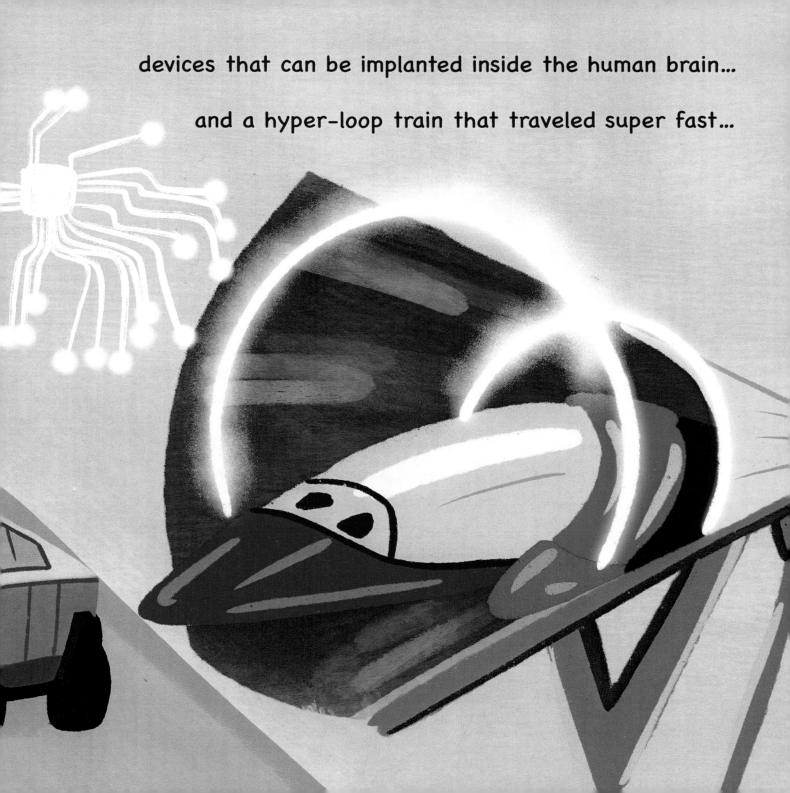

I don't know what the future holds, but I do know I'll never stop inventing.

When something is important enough, you do it even if the odds are not in your favor.

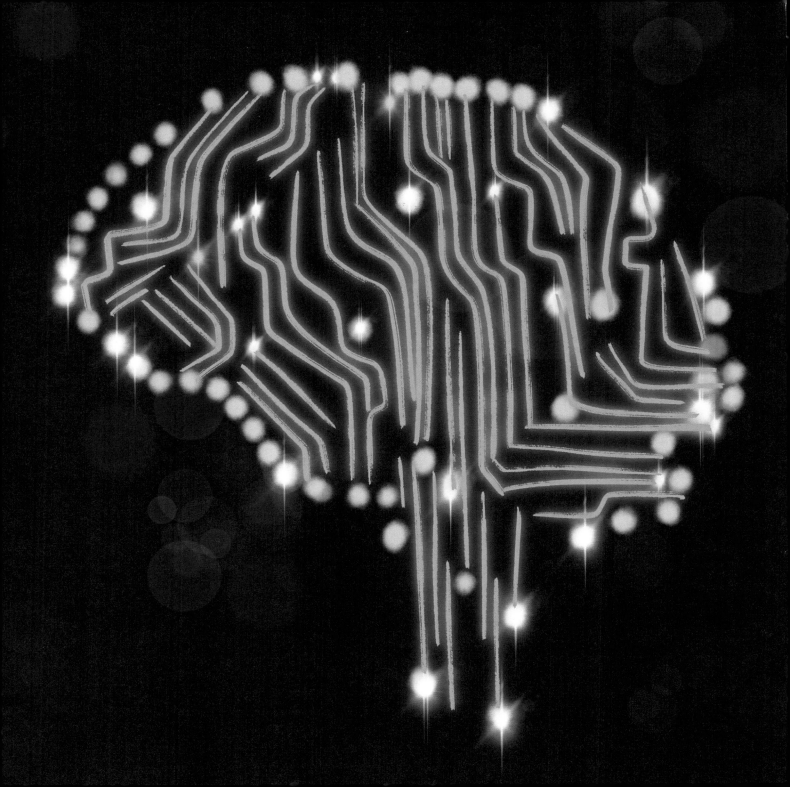

Timeline

1980 – Elon gets bullied and thrown down a staircase

1984 – Elon teaches himself how to code and invents 'Blastar'

1994 – Starts Zip2 with his brother, Kimbal

2003 – Starts SpaceX

2015 – Under Elon's leadership, Tesla releases the Model X

minimovers.tv

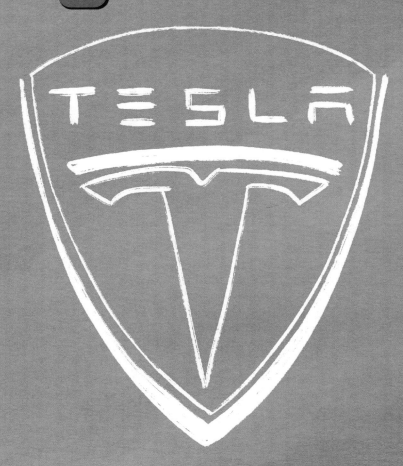

Made in United States
North Haven, CT
15 February 2023

32676070R00020